Understanding How To Raise
A Highly Sensitive Child

Everything You Need To Know To Raise Happy And Confident Children, Learn How To Manage Your Emotions To Be Heard Without Yelling

Kyla Foster

Table of Contents

Introduction

O ver the years, I have come to understand and accept that my son has anxiety and many other disorders as a result of his autism-like symptoms.

The statistics of anxiety can be overwhelming, and it can be easy to lose hope. It is important to understand that anxiety is often a temporary condition that can be resolved with help from a professional. However, parents must accept that their child may suffer from an anxiety disorder. Below are some sources and reasons that have been found to contribute to anxiety disorders.

- Genetics.
- Family history.
- Brain chemistry.
- Medications.
- Psychological stress or situational factors such as fear or previous trauma.

No one is immune to anxiety, and it can affect anyone at any age. It's always important for parents and children to monitor normal development, habits, patterns, and behaviors, as this will help them determine if their child has expressed any signs of anxiety.

In this day and age, it is almost impossible to raise a child without an anxiety disorder. Statistics show that a child who is raised with anxiety will probably have an anxiety disorder as they get older. The good news is that you can learn a lot from a child who suffers from anxiety, and your self-confidence will increase at the same time.

So, what causes an anxiety disorder? Anxiety comes about as a result of multiple sources, and it's important to deal with these sources. There are different types of anxiety that children suffer from, but some of the most common include separation anxiety, school refusal, and OCD.

Aside from what causes the fear, one of the most important things to educate your child is that you never blame them for their fears. Your child suffering from anxiety may be blaming you for things they are not capable of doing. For example, if you are missing something from their school bag when they come home, they may think that you must have taken it. Your child may also blame themselves when they do something wrong, even though they didn't do anything wrong at all.

By giving them some tools and skills at dealing with their fears, you can help them understand that their fears are actually things that have happened in the past, not things that they have done themselves or own their own actions causing the fear to happen. They will only remember your words as nothing but fear-mongering when they are older. If your child tells you there is something wrong and you tell them there's nothing wrong, it may make the situation worse in the long run. This might seem contradictory, but it's all about learning how not to be afraid.

CHAPTER 1:

Anxiety and Perfectionism

W hat do these two words have in common? They are often used interchangeably and they can both create feelings of stress, fear, or panic.

But for the most part, they are completely different emotions that manifest themselves very differently.

So, What Is the Difference?

Perfection is an emotion that can be obtained with hard work and a ton of sweat equity. Anxiety is more like a feeling of unease, and you don't feel like you can control it at all.

Perfectionism is striving for the best. Anxiety is a feeling of "not being enough" and doesn't have as much to do with what other people think. The biggest distinction that I have found between perfectionism and anxiety is that perfectionists often end up promoting their work or themselves out of a sense of false pride or over-confidence. Meanwhile, the people who experience panic attacks due to anxiety are simply trying to fit into society and cope with feelings of not being able to control those around them.

In my experience, I find perfectionists to be extremely confident about their work. They believe that the best way to grow is by hard work and doing everything they can to get the biggest return possible out of themselves.

This usually means they're willing to make sacrifices along the way and are very competitive with themselves and others. Being a perfectionist means you're willing to put yourself out there for everyone to see if it means you'll be able to grow as a person or reach success in your career. In my experience, with anxiety, you are paralyzed with fear about how other people will perceive you or your work. Unlike perfectionists, people who suffer from anxiety tend to hide from the world and wonder what everyone else is thinking about them. They don't let themselves be vulnerable because they're afraid that their flaws will come out in the open and everyone will laugh at them. This causes a cycle of wanting to put off trying new things because of fear of failure and/or looking stupid.

We all get anxious at some point. The world is unpredictable and full of uncertainty, and we can't control things that are happening right now. Sometimes, when you're feeling anxious, it can seem like your mind will never be at peace again.

It's tough to find the time or energy to do anything else while you feel this way, so it often feels better to just stay still in bed for hours on end, cut off from the world and everyone around you until the feeling subsides.

Many people find this behavior of theirs frustrating, and many others get frustrated when they can't stop themselves from this behavior. However, it isn't always the case that we are able to control our feelings in these situations. In fact, there's a good chance that you might actually want to feel anxious sometimes, and feel like bad things happening in the world that you can't control.

This is a natural human reaction to bad things happening in the world, but it isn't always the healthiest way of dealing with everything. If you have big and complicated problems, it may seem like you can't possibly get through them.

However, this isn't true. It is possible to solve any problem you face, and while they might seem impossible, it is possible that it can be solved at some point.

You might not be able to see how you'll ever accomplish these things now, and that's okay. Some days, you will feel like the thing you're trying to achieve is impossible and that it may never happen. That isn't always a negative thing, though.

Sometimes, we need to practice feeling this way so that we can know what it feels like when things are going bad and we can learn how to take control of our emotions even in the most difficult of situations.

The thing is, when you feel anxious or overwhelmed by the world, it often isn't because things are bad or dangerous. For example, you might think that you are constantly getting bullied in elementary school and that this isn't normal, but this is simply an example of something happening that you can't control and how it affects your life.

At the time, you might feel like your life is over and that this will never end, but really it won't be like this forever. It may seem impossible to believe right now, but there is always a way out of difficult situations in your life.

You just have to be able to adapt and change according to the situation at hand. Sometimes, the best way for you to deal with anxiety or depression is actually by being more active and doing things that make you happy rather than staying still in bed. It might be hard to change the way that you feel, but it isn't impossible.

As long as you have control over your emotions, exercise your mind and learn to keep an open mind, you can achieve anything that you put your mind to. The trick is just being able to do these things even when there are so many other things going on in your life right now and at the same time.

Once you've adapted to this type of learning, you'll be better able to handle the tough times in life and it will actually make it easier for you to handle anxiety in the future. It is normal to feel anxious sometimes, but that doesn't mean that there aren't ways out of these situations.

CHAPTER 2:

Anxiety and Shyness

S ome people experience a lot of anxiety in everyday situations. They may feel apprehensive about meeting new people or doing something that is outside of their normal routine, such as speaking at work or going to school. Other people are shy and may want to be more sociable but have difficulty approaching other people, particularly those they don't know very well.

This can lead to problems with relationships and feelings of loneliness. These feelings can cause severe difficulties in leading a normal life. They may feel they are socially inept and unable to cope with day-to-day social situations.

This sounds awful, doesn't it? The fact is that anxiety and shyness are common problems for many people, including young people who feel they need help with these problems in order to lead a normal life.

In this chapter, we will look at how anxiety and shyness develop in children and young people, why they arise, and what you can do about them. Psycho-social background of anxiety and shyness in children.

This type of difficulty develops when the young person does not have a good enough understanding of what is going on around them.

They may be aware of other people's thoughts and feelings, but their own thoughts and feelings are not as clear. This lack of awareness is often due to a lack of explanation from their parents about why they do or do not behave in certain ways.

Young people who are shy or anxious often have parents and guardians who are also shy and anxious. These young people may observe their parent's difficulties when facing social situations and they may learn to develop the same type of difficulties through imitation.

As a result, the young person has difficulty with friendships, school relationships, and interacting with family members.

A basic cause for anxious behavior in children is that they experience fear and discomfort when faced with new experiences or new environments. They interpret this feeling as anxiety.

A second cause is that they have difficulty in dealing with the stress of having a social problem. They feel anxious and distressed, but cannot express this clearly as it is an emotion that is more difficult to deal with.

The third factor relates to the way information about the situations they are faced with is being interpreted. The information that they are getting from their experiences may not be as clear as it should be. This can lead to feelings of anxiety that can make them feel very agitated or irritated.

Why Are Children and Young People Anxious?

Young people (and adults) who feel anxious often show evidence of this in four ways. These are:

1. Behavior to the other person.
2. Posture or body language.
3. Avoidance of situations or activities.
4. Physical reactions such as shaking.

The following examples represent how these factors affect your child or young person: A frightened child runs away from a group of friends in order to hide his/her feelings. He/she may avoid situations with new people, particularly those he/she does not know well. He/she may also show avoidance behavior when faced with his/her teacher at school.

A shy child behaves defensively or in a manner that will prevent his/her feelings from being exposed to other people. He/she may stand close to his/her parent in the classroom and look down at the floor, rather than face the person who is talking to him/her. Alternatively, he/she might choose to ignore a new group of friends altogether by dropping out of activities that involve making new friends. If confronted by another person, a shy child or teenager may display physical symptoms such as shaking or sweating in order to disguise his/her true feelings. A review of anxiety and shyness in children—features and management options.

Children's feelings are often not clearly expressed because of their lack of experience and understanding of the world around them. They are also more likely to be fearful of new situations due to their limited ability to understand how people react or feel.

Causes/Signs

The following are the most common causes/signs of anxiety and shyness in young people.

1. **Physical symptoms.** A lack of experience in social situations means that the young person cannot know what to expect. This can lead to them displaying physical symptoms such as shaking or sweating, particularly if they are talking to their parents or guardians about the problem.

2. **'Over-attachment.'** Children with this problem tend to find it difficult to say what they need and may switch from one topic of conversation to another. They may seek reassurance from their parents because of the fear that their needs are not being understood.

3. **Shyness and anxiety in children.** The following describes a range of early symptoms, including preoccupation with a situation or person.

Anxious young people can persistently turn their attention towards certain situations, especially those perceived as threatening or unfamiliar. This may mean that they spend a lot of time thinking and worrying about the situation.

They may also worry about how to handle the situation and what the outcome might be. After a while, their thought processes can become obsessive, especially when faced with situations that have aroused anxiety.

The child or young person becomes preoccupied with thinking about the situation in order to steady themselves for the experience. Such individuals can often have flashbacks or recurrent thoughts about the episodes which have caused them anxiety in the past.

How to Talk About It with Your Kid

The following are some ways in which you can help your child or young person to manage his/her anxiety.

1. Explain the reason for the anxiety.
2. Make the situation clear.
3. Take a step back and think about what might be happening and why.

4. Think about what the situation is likely to be like in reality, not just what it might be like in your imagination.

5. Read up on different situations that have caused anxiety or problems with shyness before.

6. Have a discussion with your child or young person about what makes him/her feel anxious.

7. Try to make out that the situation is not so threatening and ask him/her to tell you how he/she feels about it.

8. Ask your child or young person to think about what might happen, rather than focusing on what he/she might do or say.

9. Make sure that you are emotionally supportive towards your child or young person during the anxiety episode and reassure him/her that he/she is still loved and cared for.

The following are the most common ways in which you can make an anxious young person feel better.

1. Remind him/her that he/she is still loved and cared for.

2. Explain that many people who are anxious or shy feel this way.

3. Talk about the situation in a calm and reassuring tone, even if you are feeling worried yourself.

4. Allow your child or young person to talk about what he/she is feeling and try to reassure him/her that it is

perfectly natural to feel afraid before a new experience or challenge.

5. Explain that everyone gets anxious sometimes, even the most confident people.

6. Encourage your young person to tell you about his/her fears and worries.

7. Try to help him/her to manage his/her fears by being supportive and encouraging him/her to solve his/her own problems.

8. Do not punish or criticize your child for being shy or anxious, as this will make him/her feel worse about himself/herself.

9. Do not make a big deal out of it and avoid making your child or young person feel embarrassed about his/her anxiety or shyness.

10. Do not suggest that he/she is being difficult or unreasonable.

11. Try to get him/her to vent his/her feelings and do not try to stop him/her.

12. Give your child or young person practical advice about the steps that he/she can take towards solving his/her problems, rather than just trying to boost their confidence.

13. Encourage your child or young person in whatever he/she is doing well and praise him/her in a manner that does not make them feel self-conscious.

CHAPTER 3:

Strategies to Help Your Kids Succeed

A nxiety is an emotion that we all experience at times during the course of our lives. It is perfectly normal to feel anxious from time to time, and it typically goes away on its own. When anxiety becomes chronic or debilitating, it can be quite detrimental to a person's quality of life.

Listed below are some suggestions

- Children who are experiencing anxiety can benefit from being seen by a professional and receiving the appropriate treatment for their condition. This will hopefully provide the needed tools necessary for them to feel more in control as well as learn how they can function more easily in their everyday life.
- Help them identify triggers that trigger anxiety so that they can learn to cope with it. Unfortunately, anxiety develops as a result of certain specific triggers that we are all subjected to from time to time. These triggers can vary depending on the generation or the individual

being affected by anxiety. Each child should have a personal list of these specific triggers and should commit to working through this list with a mental health professional so that they can learn how to cope effectively with all situations that may trigger anxiety in them.

Create a stress management plan for your child. Each child should figure out his/her own unique method that he/she can use to manage his/her anxiety effectively. Some children may choose to meditate to relieve the built-up pressure in their bodies until it no longer triggers anxiety. Other children may just prefer to walk around outside during times they anticipate feeling anxious or going for a long drive with the windows rolled down so that they can feel the cool breeze blowing through their hair.

Help your child to learn how to express his/her feelings appropriately. Many children who have anxiety often suffer from being unable to communicate effectively their feelings. They may feel that they are a burden to the people around them and as a result, become more isolated with their feelings which only exacerbates the problem.

As parents, it is extremely important for us to support our children by helping them learn appropriate ways in which they can express their emotions without feeling too overwhelmed by the circumstances of their lives.

Attend family therapy sessions together. It is vital for parents to work together with their children in the process of overcoming anxiety. During family therapy sessions, you will be able to support one another and work through the triggers that may continue to cause your child anxiety or even post-traumatic stress disorder. As parents, we are the ones who can help our children to overcome their anxiety and put themselves in a better position to succeed in their everyday lives.

1. Parenting an anxious child is not easy.
2. Face anxiety. Not overprotect your kid.
3. Watch out for anger and criticism.
4. Frustration and failure to accept reality can make your life more difficult.
5. Create a bond with your kid.
6. Acknowledge your kid's feelings.
7. Give encouragement.
8. Don't reinforce the fear.
9. Help your kid to put a plan in place to manage stressful situations.
10. Pursue support.
11. It takes time, don't think it's a quick journey.
12. Constructive mindset.
13. Language/words choose.

CHAPTER 4:

Manage Anxious Kids during Travels

Kids want to be able to participate in the excitement of the season, but they can feel overstimulated and exhausted. It is important for parents to include kids in holiday traditions wherever possible, while also limiting exposure.

Here are tips on how to help your child cope with the holiday stress:

1. **Set realistic expectations for children and their parents:** Set up clear expectations of what your family wants to accomplish during the holidays.
   For example, make sure you set aside enough time each day to enjoy your family. Avoid setting high demands that can result in high-stress levels for everyone.

2. **Give children choices:** Do your best to help children feel involved by allowing them to choose activities that they want to do.

3. **Use the environment to soothe:** Keep a calm environment in your home. Play soothing music, keep

lights low, and provide plenty of outlets for your child's creative outlet (e.g., art, crafts, reading).

4. **Limit screen time:** Frequent television watching is linked to depression and anxiety disorders in children. Limiting your child's screen time can help with calming his/her stress.

5. **Encourage healthy sleep:** Sleep is an important part of coping with stressful situations.
   Make sure your child is getting enough sleep and helps him/her get to bed at a decent time.

Some typical signs that your child may be feeling anxious or overwhelmed are:

- Nervous habits: biting nails, running fingers through hair (pulling it out), or rubbing hands together.
- Avoidance: saying no when asked to do something or just not responding.
- Fatigued: difficulty falling asleep or staying asleep throughout the night; tired during the day.
- Overreacting: easily startled; crying at the drop of a hat.
- Eating problems: eating too much and then vomiting.
- Aggressive: hitting, throwing objects, or hitting siblings or parents.
- Irritability: getting angry easily; yelling and complaining a lot.

If your child is overstimulated and you have no idea what they need, try these coping strategies: Jumping up and down, wide-open, or arms outstretched if the need to be entertained strikes. Jumping up and down and dancing your way through the holiday decorating can work wonders.

Have fun by reciting a Christmas wish list to your child over and over until it becomes etched in his/her memory. You might also want to play a game that requires him/her to do certain tasks, such as getting his/her hands dirty, then move on to another task.

This will allow him/her to take control of the situation so he/she does not feel overwhelmed by what he/she is unable or unwilling to do.

Tuck your child in bed with a fun Christmas story on Christmas Eve and read it again the next morning. Start early, so your child has plenty of time to get comfortable with the idea.

"If you feel overwhelmed by insane holiday stress, don't hesitate to reach out for help. Call a friend, a support group, or mental health professional, and be sure to listen closely to his/her advice.

If a professional is not the right fit for you or your child, consider finding a therapist who works with children. Be sure to ask about his/her experience with working with families and listen carefully to his/her suggestions for how to handle any tricky situations."

Carey Downfield, M.D., medical director of psychiatric services at the Children's Hospital of Philadelphia's Office of Psychiatry and Related Diseases.

"The holidays can be an overwhelming time for kids and parents alike, but there are ways to help your child cope with this stress. Here are a few tips for minimizing holiday stress for kids:

1. Let go of your expectations about what your family will or won't be doing over the holidays, including the type of activities they will do (family traditions or staying home alone).

2. Enable your children to feel like they are part of the festivities by giving them a chance to help with the preparation and decoration.

3. Use a calming environment that is free from excessive noise or lights by having soothing music and dimmed lights available when you want to settle down and relax together as a family."

CHAPTER 5:

How to Approach Extended Family & Teachers

Here are some tips from my kid and others anxious kid's experiences:

1. "I have severe anxiety. I've been fighting it for many years, and it's really tough. It's even tougher when my mom goes on long trips for work—so I thought of some ways to help me cope. I hope you find them helpful."

2. My mom is gone for two weeks, I get kind of anxious and I can't really rest at night.

   Because she is gone, I am kind of worried about my sister, because she doesn't have any adult to take care of her if something happens (I know she's old enough to take care of herself, but when you're not used to doing certain stuff, it's really hard. Even when my mom is at home, I still get anxious, because she works a lot and I think that she will forget about me).

3. It might be a kind of mean, but here's what I do when I'm down and need to rest. My friends know that I have anxiety and they know how to act around me—so in this

situation, they help me get rest. When my mom is gone, we just play video games, watch movies or just chill no matter the weather. I will be really happy that I can just play video games without thinking anything about my mom or my sister. Even if I don't feel like playing games, they force me to hang out with them and drink some tea (that's what I always drink when I'm nervous).

4. When you have a family member gone, it might be hard to adjust to a new lifestyle—everybody needs to change a bit. I'm kind of used to my mom being around all the time, but now it's just me and my sister. When it's time to eat, I ask her if she wants to buy food or cook - most of the time she says that we should cook. Now that I think about it, I'm not really a fan of cooking ha-ha.

5. You can maybe try to find other ways to occupy your time. I try to go outside a lot, take a walk, clean the house—you know, stuff I don't really do when my mom is at home. It's easier for me to do that when she's away.

6. When your anxiety reaches a point of no return, you just have to talk about it. You have to know how you're feeling before going through an anxiety attack. If you're not sure what to do—just talk about it with someone.

   Your friends, a family member, it doesn't really matter. The best thing about talking is that you will be able to feel better, you will be able to explain how you're feeling and the surrounding people will be able to help.

7. If your mom is at home, that means she's not far from you, even if she's not physically with you. If you ever have any problems, you can ask her for help or even call her and talk with her. If she's not at home, that means that she's really far from you and it'll be hard to get in touch with her all the time. That's why when my mom is away I prepare myself and I know what to do if something bad happens. It might be a good idea to make a list of things that need to be done—just in case. For example, I know that my mom has to go to work, but I'm never sure when her shift starts, and I don't want to wake up and find out she's gone at the wrong time. That's why I prepare a list of things that need to be done if something happens.

8. When I have anxiety, I always feel really tired and can't do anything. It's as if you were about to sleep but couldn't, so you just lay down and stare at the ceiling. That's how you feel with anxiety, but worse. When my mom is away I find it hard to get rest, but sometimes some things make me anxious all day long—even though they're not related to my mom (for example, talking with a new person). When that happens, I just think about them and make a mental list of things I need to do. For example, this one time my mom was gone for 4 days, and she was about to come home—but that day I had an anxiety attack. It's because this one girl called me fat

34

even though she wasn't—it sounds stupid, but it really hurt me. My mom was gone for 4 days and I didn't talk with her all that time—plus the fact that the girl hurtled my feeling. Because of that, I felt really anxious and I couldn't sleep.

So I thought about the girl, made a list, and told myself not to have those kinds of thoughts. I didn't want to think about the list, just telling my brain what to do - it sounds weird, but I'm kind of used to do that now.

9. When your mom is away, you can get some space for yourself and make a plan of what you need to do. For example, if you want to save money, a good idea could be giving up eating out or something like that. I don't know how that works, but it's good to think about how you can save money.

10. Try to go out with your friends or see movies alone. You just need to do whatever makes you feel better, and not be alone all the time.

    For example, if I miss my mom, I try to make plans with other people and go out with them for as long as possible—what I mean by that is going to the movies or a nice restaurant.

    It feels good to have an idea of what you need to do and to feel like you're not alone.

11. Try to exercise every day—that helps you relax, have better sleep, and be more confident.

12. Start a journal right now—it's another method that helps keep track of your anxiety attacks/situations—plus it makes writing things easier for you in the future.

13. If you're using any kind of medication, try not to depend on it. My mom is a nurse, and she said that some people can become super dependent on meds—so I try not to use them all the time, and use them only when I really need to.

    It's good to try and use other methods than medications, too.

14. Trust your anxiety. It might sound kind of weird, but trust me, it works. I know some people don't believe in that, but trust me: if you feel bad because you want to be home with your mom, or because you feel like something bad is going to happen—just go with it. Trust your anxiety and let those feelings go.

The idea of spending time with extended family can be intimidating, but the holidays can be a perfect opportunity to make new memories and strengthen bonds.

In order to avoid the dreaded defensiveness that often happens when dealing with difficult people, it's important to remember these few things:

- **Be yourself.** Let your personality shine through and don't worry if you're not meeting expectations. It's better for people to have a genuine experience than an artificial one. Be kind, be patient, and don't take anything too seriously.

- **Don't overdo it on the food & take an extra snack with you.** Enjoy the holiday fare, but keep your portions reasonable so you can avoid digestive issues and bloat.

- **Keep a positive attitude.** Keep your thoughts focused on gratitude, compassion, and love. If family or friends are lacking in these areas, or are behaving negatively, kindly ask them to stop. Have a kind heart and know that it's okay to say "no."

- **Get relaxed and enjoy yourself with your family.** This may be the only time of year where everyone can hang out at the same time, so make good use of it. It's nice to be together and get to know each other more deeply despite any misgivings.

- **Don't 'over-prepare.'** Keep in mind that people are most likely going to bring their own plans to the holiday meal and not everyone is going to follow your plan.

No matter what you're up against, try to be at least a little bit reasonable and understanding. Remind yourself that people at times do things we don't understand. If they are being uncommunicative or distant, try to keep your feelings towards them in their best light and appreciative. Try to avoid taking it personally. Try to remember that there are a lot of factors that can influence people's actions and moods, even when they might be bad. Try to put your feelings into perspective and know that every person has their own story and journey. Having a positive attitude and being friendly goes a long way towards avoiding being overwhelmed or frustrated.

No matter how truly awful your family, friends or partner may be at any given time, try to remember that everyone is entitled to their limits or feelings. Just don't let your issues get in the way of how to act. It's actually a wonderful opportunity to make new friends, strengthen old friendships, and learn more about yourself and others.

CHAPTER 6:

Help Kids Manage Anxiety during the Pandemic

A s the pandemic progresses, more and more parents are becoming concerned about how their children are responding to the ever-changing news.

Some children will be no less anxious than they were before, while others may respond by suddenly feeling much better or worse.

There is a great deal of variability in how kids react to the pandemic news.

And there may also be a wide range in how the kids feel and/or behave after the news, even within the same family.

Many parents are asking for advice on how to help their children cope with the imminent pandemic. Several books have been written about how to manage anxieties during a crisis.

The problem is that not all situations are alike, and not all people respond uniformly to any situation.

Most of these books also reflect a scientific model of how children react to the news.

Combatting Anxiety in Your Children

It is good to start with the basics and take it up from there. This means ensuring that you and your children are exposed to the basics of care. These include:

Getting the Right Amount of Sleep

No matter what, you should never meddle with sleep time. Your children need the right amount of sleep to aid their emotional wellbeing and help their brain function optimally. This is not for children and adolescents only, but includes people of all ages. You know how you feel when you're running on little to no sleep. You get exhausted, irritable, and unable to stay alert as usual while increasing the risks of exhibiting depressive symptoms. Now, that's for you, the adult. So, imagine how your children will react to a lack of sleep mixed in with anxiety. This will only affect the important physiological processes necessary for their maturation. Activate the right sleep hygiene measures, which will ensure optimal sleep.

These include:

- Exposing your kids to as much natural light as possible during the day.
- Eliminating spicy or fatty foods just before bedtime.
- No caffeinated drinks.
- No screens emitting blue light, including TV, laptops, or smartphones, an hour before bedtime.

- Use the perfect room temperature.
- Stick to a regular bedtime schedule.
- For parents, you should make sure that you have no coffee or other caffeinated drinks late in the evening. When I say attend to the basics, you are not left out too.
- Implement the precautions.
- Note for any sign of illness in your children.

Exercise

Engage in regular physical activity with your children. This shouldn't be anything too complicated but age-appropriate enough to maintain their physical wellness.

Don't Be Afraid to Seek Professional Help

If you ever have a reason to believe at some point that your child has a mental health condition, it is okay to seek professional help. There are many helplines available with professionals who can guide you on the right steps to take. You may miss the symptoms of childhood anxiety at first because you erroneously thought that they would outgrow the "bizarre" behavior.

However, as you realize that this is anxiety, it is important that you don't believe that this should be left to you alone. It is okay to get some psychological support as well as you need to be at optimal mental health to offer the needed guidance and support for your children with anxiety.

Attending to the Basics

Here are tips that will help you bring some semblance of normalcy in your home as you try to calm the anxiety in your children:

Provide Some Structure to the Day

There is so much unpredictability in these times, and your day shouldn't be too. A day with no clear schedule can contribute to the high level of anxiety in your home among your children and teens. So, help your children feel some sense of agency and accomplishment by having a definite daily schedule. For parents working from home, you can do this in such a way that it doesn't encroach on your work time. Be sure not to go overboard with the scheduling, as it is beneficial to do this in moderation. When it's too restrictive, you could be sitting on a time bomb as well. Be flexible with the schedule, but keep the wake-up time and bedtime as regular as possible.

Pick Your Battles

While this may be from a place of love, a lot of parents give in to the urge to correct every single move of their child that they consider annoying. At this point, you will have to pick your battles and focus more on positive feedback. Since these children will be home with you for more hours than usual, this will only amplify negative feelings in your home. So, try to disengage from this action. Instead of picking out every single time they mess up or are "annoying," you should praise their desirable behavior. This shouldn't be general, but a little more specific to show that you are paying attention. Also, you need to be able to tell the difference between an annoying behavior and a dangerous one. The annoying behavior may just be your child trying to cope with the situation in the way they know how to and could be completely unintentional. You will only reinforce the undesirable behavior when you pay more attention to it. Negative criticism and feedback shouldn't be too constant, as it will only ruin your child's self-esteem.

Prioritize Spending Quality Time Together

Your schedule should include activities you can participate in with your children. Even as little as twenty minutes of quality time spent with your children regularly will go a long way. These children will feel calmer, understood, and supported as they see how much you're willing to go to create time for them. Your activities should be age-appropriate. For example, those below ten years of age would put a different meaning to quality time compared to those above that age range. You can use freely chosen play or child-directed play for the younger age group. This simply means letting the child be in charge of the direction of the play rather than giving instructions or telling him/her exactly what to do.

Practice Mindfulness

This is more for you than for your children. It's okay to take a few minutes to pause and slow down. You can do this through mindful pauses during the day. This will offer assistance to both you and your child with a progressed passionate wellbeing level, as you'll be able to recapture point of view amid those overpowering times.

You're more likely not to flip out when you're already in a state of calm. With mindfulness, you can be more effective at practicing better parenting during the pandemic by being less reactive and more patient.

Let Your Children Take up Hobbies

Now is a good time to put hobbies on the schedule. While schoolwork is important, you shouldn't neglect the creative part of your children that is necessary for their developing brain. It could be literally anything that you know would add value to their lives and help them find some purpose during this pandemic. There is a lot of free time now anyway, so no excuses. You could encourage them to get started on activities such as reading, painting, drawing, writing, dancing, singing, or playing a musical instrument. Now that you're home with them, you can encourage your children to explore their creativity. This will give them a sense of joy and fulfillment, which is important for their cognitive and emotional wellbeing in the long run.

Limit the Use of Media

You don't have to monitor actively the number of coronavirus cases and deaths every day. This is not only bad for your children, but could put a severe dent in your mental health as well. As you expose them to that horrible news, it could be confusing, scary, and exhausting for your children. While it's okay to stay up-to-date on happenings around you, this should be limited to as little as possible based on the developmental level and age of your children. You will realize that the household feels calmer when you're not watching every day as people lose their lives. This should not be confused with shielding them from what's going on. They deserve to know without being kept in the dark. When explaining to them what is happening on the news, be as factual as possible.

Keep Them Connected with Friends

One of the hallmarks of the novel coronavirus is that we are unable to physically meet with friends and family. This social isolation could be disastrous for children, as they have to get used to the fact that they can't leave home as much as they want. They can't hug their friends or engage in those activities they most likely took for granted. You can follow the guidelines stipulated by the CDC by taking advantage of the technology at your fingertips. Organize video chat sessions where they can connect with their friends using their social media accounts, smartphones, or laptops. The teens will most likely have social media accounts, and you can supervise this minimally to ensure that they are using it appropriately.

Engage Them in Developmentally Appropriate Tasks

Let them do things for themselves in situations where you know they can handle it. You can entrust them with the tasks of cleaning up paint after painting, putting their crayons back, folding laundry, or rolling out the dough. These are all developmentally appropriate tasks that will help them gain confidence, agency, and a sense of mastery. You can also get them in on the simple household activity. For teenagers, you can encourage them to help their younger siblings with their learning activities. They can also help you shop online for groceries and other essentials. Remember to supervise and monitor these tasks to avoid putting your child in harm's way.

Stay Calm, Listen, and Offer Reassurance

You are your child's role model, and they will be actively learning from the example you show. Be sure to react as calmly as possible to situations as your children will respond to your reactions. So, how do you talk about COVID-19 when you think they are not listening? Save the serious conversations for when you're sure they are not lurking around. You don't want to increase your children's fear unnecessarily. You also don't want to decrease it in such a way that they have no regard for their personal safety. Be sure to remind your children that you are all healthy and reassure them that you will continue to ensure that they are all safe and well during the pandemic. This is also a good time to encourage them to write out their feelings while you respond as truthfully as possible.

Encourage Them to Help Others

This is a good time to take them on a lesson in empathy. You can identify projects that will help others around you and encourage your children to participate. These can be tasks as little as writing letters to your neighbors that are stuck at home alone.

You can even encourage them to send messages of hope to healthcare workers or other positive messages on social media. Just as you're feeling a little blue with the current situation, your children can talk with others and draw strength from each other.

CHAPTER 7:

Anxious Feelings Are Real and Severe

As you consider your child's Fear issue, we have to disperse one dangerous misconception. Everybody has anxiety. This reality makes it simple for individual's unafraid issues to contrast their very own nerves with the encounters of individuals experiencing tremendous, neurotic anxiety. In this misinformed view, individuals without a Fear issue are emotionally "solid," and those with a Fear issue are emotionally "frail."

The mistake here is in not understanding that these encounters of fear are distinctive in degree as well as various in kind. The individual enduring a fear issue has truly awkward sentiments. What's more, numerous individuals with fear create convictions that the peril caution going off in their cerebrums must reflect genuine outside threat, even though they realize that others don't see risk in comparative circumstances. The individual who fears being caught in a lift realizes that other individuals don't fear lifts; all things considered, he/she accepts that he/she will be found and unfit to take in a stuck elevator.

After some time, this example of neurotic fear increases, isolating the anxious individual from the individuals who don't have fear issues. Try not to accept that your fear resembles your anxious child's experience, except if you additionally experience the ill effects of a genuine fear issue. Making that suspicion will undermine your capacity to support your child. He/she will imagine that you don't comprehend his/her experience and that you consider him/her to be feeble or insufficient.

Late research has indicated that fear disorders are the most well-known mental disorders in children, with around one of every eight children being influenced. This is more than double the rate for temperament disorders, including wretchedness and bipolar disorder. Fear disorders, by and large, are more typical of young ladies than in young men. Children with a parent who has fear are on multiple occasions as prone to have this issue themselves, just like those children whose guardians didn't have a fear disorder.

Fear appears as emotions, contemplations, and practices identified with the risk of the threat, even though this outside peril is little or nonexistent. The foreseen threat isn't outside of the anxious child; it is inside. The expectation of encountering this unpleasant inclination produces upsetting contemplations and avoidant practices. Fear is the cerebrum's robust, valuable caution flagging risk when there is no sensible outer danger. Fear is a bogus caution in your child's sensory system. It is genuine and painful. It is particularly upsetting to a child who comes up short on a grown-up comprehension of Fear issues.

Fear in children is typically found in practices that reflect concern and the requirement for insurance, consolation, and break. Fear issues appear as gaps in the child's life. The child dodges certain things since he/she fears the terrible emotions that anxiety produces.

At moderately low levels and in proper circumstances, fear can be valuable to a child; however, this happens when no genuine outer threat is available, it isn't useful. Feeling a low degree of fear, fully expecting a test at school, is healthy. However, an elevated level of anxiety may make it outlandish for a child to step through the examination or even go to class that day.

This isn't healthy; it is probably going to be a Fear issue. Anxious grown-ups, just as anxious children, understand that their emotions are strange, so they frequently conceal the reasons they don't get things done, to escape individuals' analysis.

All things being equal, grown-ups ordinarily articulate their sentiments of fear. Children are more outlandish than adults to state, "I'm anxious" or "I'm concerned" and are bound to showcase their fear by changing their conduct—for instance, by not going to class or not remaining medium-term with a companion.

Children are more probable than grown-ups to show fear by griping about the disease, particularly migraines and stomach hurts, since they rapidly discover that physical issues can assist them with staying away from circumstances that may create anxiety, such as going to class or stepping through an exam.

You realize your child has a fear issue when you see maladaptive practices—for the most part, shirking practices that are the consequence of the "flight" part of the battle or flight reaction to looming apparent perils. Sticking to grown-ups, particularly guardians, and declining to go to new or new places are primary indications of fear in more youthful children. More seasoned anxious children are bound to shroud their fear by essentially saying, "I would prefer not to do it," when looked at things that make them anxious. Now and again, more seasoned children participate in troublesome conduct to escape things they don't like.

However, this isn't basic among anxious youths because they are typically trustworthy about staying away from analysis from grown-ups in power, for example, guardians and educators.

As a parent, you need your child to make the most of the plentiful open doors that life offers. At the point when your anxious child pulls once again from ordinary educational encounters, this is an indication that he/she may have a Fear issue. Even though fear is unitary, the practices that show fear fluctuate, thus do the triggers of anxiety for singular children.

What makes one anxious child horrendously irritated will be no issue at all for another anxious child. Explicit fear activating circumstances and conduct reactions to these make a specific anxious child's examples of anxiety. These ruinous examples are reflected in the six center fear disorders, which are depicted later in this part.

Even though this book is intended for children who have fear issues yet don't experience the ill effects of fear disorders, by and by, it's useful for guardians to comprehend the six specific fear disorders. Along these lines, the child's fear issues can be described, and guardians can contemplate what should be finished.

Children who have untreated fear disorders are bound to have an assortment of different issues, regularly later in their lives— with sadness during youthful adulthood being exceptionally healthy.

How Anxiety Affects People Who Live with It as a Parent

Anxiety impacts people in different ways, which is why it can be so challenging to deal with, as not every case is the same.

The symptoms of anxiety can vary depending on each individual case, so identifying anxiety in yourself and knowing when it has become problematic ultimately depends on your personal feeling towards your symptoms. If you feel like you truly cannot get them under control by yourself or like they are negatively impacting your quality of life, chances are, and you are dealing with problematic anxiety that needs to be treated properly.

If you are experiencing overwhelming anxiety on an ongoing basis, you might find that you are constantly feeling restless and overwhelmed, even when there are no real reasons for you to feel anxious. This feeling of restlessness may come and go randomly for no apparent reason, or it may be constant if you are dealing with a more advanced case of problematic anxiety disorder. When you feel this restlessness, it may feel like every little thing can lead to you having a full-blown panic attack or intense anxiety developing around seemingly minor things. For example, you may be driving in your car and need to pass a slow driver, and the act of switching lanes and passing that slow driver may cause you to experience intense anxiety. Or maybe you are sitting on your couch and you hear a loud bang from your family in the other room and your heart rate skyrockets and you have a momentary feeling like you need to run and save yourself. These types of restlessness and responses can be extremely overwhelming and problematic and can leave you feeling like you constantly have to be prepared to have an intense response to a minor thing because it feels uncontrollable.

In addition to intense responses, you may also feel constant feelings of worrying thoughts in your mind, even if you cannot logically back up your worry with rational or reasonable reasons as to why. You may feel like you are constantly worried about things, even if you can logically understand why these feelings of worry are invalid or unlikely to manifest as being true.

Every time you do have a reason to worry, then you might find yourself having an intense stress-related response because you were already in a heightened state of worry in the first place. As a result, it may feel like you are never able to relax and experience rest or calm because you are constantly overwhelmed and stressed out.

Due to your constant state of anxiety and worry, you may also find yourself being highly irritable and moody. It is actually not uncommon for people with anxiety to experience intense anger, which is essentially a natural "fight" response from the fight-or-flight mode. You may find that in most cases you want to run away, but in cases where you cannot or where you feel like you are caught by surprise instead, you get angry. You might find yourself yelling, arguing with others, or simply holding onto feelings of intense anger and resentment on an ongoing basis because of the anxiety disorder that you live with.

Other symptoms of anxiety include concentration difficulties and sleep difficulties. As a result of your body constantly producing so much cortisol and adrenaline, it may feel like you are having a hard time paying attention or making up your mind about things. Engaging in basic conversations may be challenging, and it may feel like you cannot stay focused on one task for longer than a few minutes at a time.

You may also find like your stress leaks over into your sleep and that you cannot sleep soundly each night, making it challenging for you to feel well-rested. Alternatively, you may find yourself so stressed out that all you want to do is sleep because it feels as though your time spent sleeping is the only peaceful time that you have. The constant stress may make it feel like you are chronically exhausted, whether you have slept too much or too little, which can leave you feeling uncomfortable and frustrated all the time.

CHAPTER 8:

Will a Highly Sensitive Child Present the Same Anxiety Level Forever?

A s was already mentioned, anxiety is a progressive condition. It can begin as a mild form, causing minor concerns.

Parents might even ignore the problem, believing it will disappear on its own. Or, they might fail to notice anxiety is even an issue, saying that their child is just shy or has an introverted personality.

The thing to remember is that anxiety will continue to progress, especially if the root cause is not addressed. The symptoms will become more frequent and persistent, affecting both emotional and physical health.

At first, the child will avoid certain situations or people, but, in case of severe anxiety, avoidance might be generalized.

Severe anxiety does not appear overnight, and it is almost always the result of a traumatic event or situation. It is our responsibility as parents to look after our children and take the right measures to remedy anxiety. This is a treatable condition, particularly when identified at an early age.

Just as anxiety can progress from mild to moderate and severe, it is important to remember that it can go back as well. With therapy and self-help measures, the child can experience only mild anxiety and live the best quality of life. Parents should not force the child to get over his/her anxiety, as this too can negatively influence the recovery process.

Am I making my child's anxiety worse? Your child suffers from anxiety. As a parent, the one thing you want to do is support him/her. You need to teach your child to confront his/her anxiety while remaining calm and positive.

Many parents find it difficult to handle their anxious child, often making the problem worse, rather than alleviate any negative feelings. Moreover, they might be tempted to dismiss their child's emotions, complicating the issue even further.

Parents are not responsible for fixing their child, but this does not mean they should not try to be supportive. Children need their parents to respond to their anxious thoughts and behaviors healthily. In this way, they will feel guided towards the best coping strategies, and less inclined to give in to their anxiety.

Always remember that your child needs to be loved and protected, especially when dealing with anxiety. It does not matter how anxious he/she is, he/she still needs you to be there for him/her and provide the necessary support on the road toward feeling better.

Recognizing Anxiety in Other People

If your loved one is experiencing anxiety, the signs of their anxiety and the symptoms they experience will be fairly simple to identify. Typically, you can tell if someone else is experiencing anxiety based on their mannerisms and the way that they approach the world around them. If someone is experiencing anxiety, typically they will show it in their body language, their verbal language, and their actions, thoughts, and decisions.

If your loved one is experiencing anxiety, it is important that you take the time to understand what they are going through and have compassion for them and their experiences, as anxiety can be a challenging thing for anyone to navigate. Having your acceptance and understanding around their experiences is going to be extremely helpful not only in allowing them to manage their own emotional wellbeing but also in helping you both manage your relationship together.

A big sign that your friend or loved one is living with anxiety is that he/she seems on edge all the time. His/her body may seem jittery or he/she may fidget a lot when he/she is in a situation that is making him/her uncomfortable and it may seem as though his/her jitters or fidgeting are uncontrollable. Likely, your friend does not even know that he/she is doing this, but instead, he/she does it subconsciously as he/she tries to deal with his/her growing energy inside of him/her that is telling him/her that there is something wrong.

He/she may also seem jumpy or like he/she scares easily, which can make it seem like he/she is constantly living in a state of fear. This may or may not be obvious, depending on how high functioning he/she is alongside their anxiety.

Another common sign that your loved one is living with anxiety is the complaint of aches and pains, especially when it comes to complaints around chest pains. In some situations, these may be indicative of a larger problem, but in people with anxiety, chest pains are extremely common and do not typically have any medical reason behind why they are happening.

If your loved one's pulse is racing and they start experiencing chest pains as a result of this, chances are, they are experiencing fairly intense anxious responses and they need to seek professional help if they have not already.

While some people with anxiety have what is known as "high functioning anxiety" and are able to hide their symptoms, others are not able to and will openly voice their fears or concerns around things in their life. Often, their fears or concerns will seem rather grandiose or misplaced, making those around them wonder why they are so afraid of something seemingly small. Even if they are high functioning, they will likely voice their fears or concerns, except they will likely do it in a way that makes their fears seem smaller than they actually are. Often, they will voice these feelings in passing, try to minimize them with their language, or voice them as if they are a joke so that they can brush it off if anyone asks them if they are serious about how they are feeling.

Another common sign that can easily be seen by yourself or others who are observing your loved one who may be experiencing anxiety is the need to have things done in a very specific way. Anxious people often find that they need to have some form of control over everything around them as this supports them in feeling like there will be no "surprises" or unexpected turn of events. By making sure that the actions they take and sometimes the actions of those around them are done in a very specific way, the person with anxiety feels like they are in control over their lives. Anytime something does not go according to "plan," they may seem very distraught and overwhelmed, possibly having a large emotional reaction to the experience that may even seem beyond reasonable. If this is happening, there is a very likely chance that your loved one is experiencing anxiety and is not attempting to be controlling or inconsiderate, but instead is simply trying to control themselves and their experience. In other words, this is not their way of trying to make you feel bad, but instead, it is their way of trying to make themselves feel good.

CHAPTER 9:

Why a Highly Sensitive Child Suffers from Anxiety

Causes of Anxiety

As a conscious parent, you need to know what your child is going through so you can empathize with his/her feelings and emotions.

With that in mind, prepare yourself by understanding the causes and characteristics of anxiety so you can be ready for any questions or concerns your child may have.

Anxiety occurs for a variety of emotional, biological, and environmental reasons. It is built on interrelated factors, including genetics, temperament, brain chemistry, home environment, trauma, and stress.

Learning about the underlying causes of your child's individual anxiety will help you to understand what he/she is experiencing.

Focusing on the causes of behavior, rather than the behavior itself, will help you to empathize with your child so you can work together to overcome anxiety.

Psychological Aspects

Feelings in the Family

Growing up in a family where fear, worry, and anxiety are consistently modeled by parents or family members may teach a child to be anxious.

In addition, if a child grows up in a home where a parent or sibling is terminally ill, in an abusive or alcoholic home where he/she is walking on eggshells around a parent, or constantly in an over-alert state, he/she may learn to expect the worst, or actually look for the worst. The child ends up living in a state of a constant worry.

The psychological state of fear and trauma can also be present when a child is bullied at school, in the neighborhood, or on the school bus. The continuous state of anxiety that results in creates children who might freeze up or withdraw in order to protect themselves. They tend to lose their sense of belonging and separate themselves from friends.

A typical example is a child who is standing off on his/her own during lunch or recess. It is also common for a child feeling anxiety to fall into a world of his/her own where he/she might feel he/she has to create plans for how to safeguard himself, "just in case."

When this happens, the body and mind's resources are sidetracked, and your child's growth may become interrupted.

Internal versus External Stressors

The term internal refers to the vulnerability that comes from genetics and temperament. It also means how your child feels inside about what happens externally or around him/her. Internal triggers are more likely to affect a child who has strong emotions or who has a tendency to be a sensitive child.

External influences are events that happen outside of the child and have a separate point of origin. Examples of some external triggers are divorce, violence at home, school, games or TV, injury, illness or death of a family member, abuse, or a disaster.

The amount of anxiety your child feels from these triggers will be based on how he/she processes it. Therefore, it will be important for you to take the time to help your child separate out what is a real threat external to his/her from what he/she is creating internally through his/her own thoughts.

Biological Aspects

Neurotransmitters

A person's brain is a network of billions of nerve cells called neurons that communicate with each other to create thoughts, emotions, and behaviors. This process is called cell-to-cell communication, in which a transfer of information from one part of the brain to another is made possible by chemicals called neurotransmitters. The two primary neurotransmitters that affect your child's feelings are serotonin and dopamine.

The Amygdala and Hippocampus

When the fight-or-flight response is triggered, it occurs in the parts of the brain called the amygdala and hippocampus. The amygdala is the part of the brain where feelings and emotions are based. So if your child is feeling fearful and anxious, the amygdala will send this information throughout your child's body on an alert. The hippocampus holds memory, time, and place, especially for highly emotional situations. Once the amygdala jumps into action, your child can become overly sensitive to certain stimuli. It may seem like your child is consumed with worry at the moment; however, it is likely your child is revisiting the emotion of worry from the past, meaning that at some point in his/her life he/she might have experienced worry and this has been stored away in the brain and body. Parents who spend time analyzing and evaluating past events to look for clues for how worry may have surfaced are likely to enter the worry cycle themselves.

Genetic Causes

Investigations into the causes of anxiety are clear that anxiety, panic, and depression can be hereditary, and that anxiety is usually a concern for several members of the same family. If a parent or sibling has a history of anxiety or depression, a child's risk increases four-to-six-fold for developing symptoms himself/herself. This is because the structure of the brain and its processes are inherited. However, solid evidence is emerging that not only can you change your brain but also your DNA (genetic makeup). Reflections on awareness and attention show that the current generation can influence what is passed on to futures generations. Families with patterns of anxiety can now take comfort in the knowledge that the cycle of unnecessary worry can truly be broken. People who have no family history of the disorder can develop anxiety as well. Knowing your family history helps you and any professionals supporting you make clear, conscious decisions about what steps to take.

The Role of Temperament

The brain is constantly changing. It will refuge neural pathways and connections based on the information it receives, changing itself in order to learn and respond. It is a work in progress and becomes stronger through repetition and time.

Parents who are more successful in reducing their child's fearfulness and anxiety will allow the child to face fears and work through them so the preferred pathways can become stronger. It is best to challenge your child in small increments, no matter how uncomfortable, while being encouraging and loving. The good news is that temperament and personality are not fixed. They can and will be altered to your child's benefit as he/she learns to integrate coping and release strategies into his/her daily life.

Environmental Factors

Life Events

It is common when children start school or daycare, or transition to a new grade, for them to become emotional, scared, or clingy for a brief period. Usually, parents will find a few weeks are normal for the transition and are able to hang in there.

It is when the reaction becomes protracted and your child cannot move past his/her feelings about the incident that intervention will be necessary. Some common examples of stressful life events (which are external stressors) are:

- A trauma.
- Seeing violence at home, school, or on TV.
- School issues.
- Divorce.
- Moving.
- Loss.
- Anxious, overprotective, or critical parenting style.
- Difficulty with friendships.
- Death of a family member, friend, or family pet.
- Uncertainty.

When a situation lacks a clear outcome, your child might feel a lack of control and significant stress. Uncertain as to what type of coping response will be needed to deal with a particular situation, your child might be convinced he/she does not have what it takes to get through it, especially when he/she remembers difficulties he/she had in the past.

Children can learn how to manage environmental stressors by watching parents, siblings, friends, teachers, and peers at school.

If they observe people who respond to stressful situations with uncertainty, worry, nervousness, extreme caution, and overemphasis on danger, this can influence how they will react, and create a pessimistic worldview.

Parental Influence

To begin with, it is imperative to note that most guardians don't cause their children to be on edge; or maybe they unwittingly offer assistance to propagate it. I say most parents because this statement does not hold true if there is intentional violence or abuse in the home. Sometimes in your effort to do the best you can with what you have been taught or know, you are unaware that your efforts might be hindering your children.

For example, if your seven-year-old child is afraid to make new friends, you might "help" him/her by making the phone call to set up a playdate instead of assuring him/her he/she can get through it on his/her own.

Parents can also affect how a child chooses to cope with his/her anxiety by watching the choices they make. For illustration, in case you come domestic from work pushed, does your child see you reach for a glass of wine to unwind? Do you yell at others and then say, "Sorry, I had a stressful day?"

Trauma

An early traumatic experience can block the normal growth and development of coping skills, and affect your child's emotional and social growth. At the time of the event, intense feelings of fear and helplessness can overcome your child, causing him/her to feel he/she cannot think clearly or function well. If your child has experienced a life event that is outside the realm of normal human experience and the associated anxiety continues over time, even with your care, concern, and discussions with him/her, you may want to consult with your medical provider. Please note that some symptoms of anxiety may not occur at the time of the event. Also, if your child has ever experienced a panic attack and continues to avoid the place it was experienced, he/she is more likely to grow and learn from the experience if you seek professional help from a licensed provider. When help is delayed, it can complicate and/or prolong treatment.

Food

If your child is malnourished or regularly eats foods containing excess sugar, additives, or caffeine, he/she may experience anxiety, feelings of panic, an inability to sleep, night frights, and/or depression. Improper nutrition can influence your child's thought processes by altering his/her ability to concentrate or learn new material; it can also lower his/her level of awareness, weaken the growth process of his/her brain, and even increase the duration and intensity of a cold.

Because anxiety affects blood sugar levels, it can cause sensitivities and stomach problems such as pain, a bloated or distended stomach, discomfort, indigestion, and symptoms of hyperglycemia and hypoglycemia. When your child overeats, especially sweets and desserts, it can affect his/her nervous system.

This can trigger moodiness, anxiousness, sleepiness, or depression. Some people have released their anxiety almost completely through a reduction of sugary or caffeinated foods and drinks.

Sleep

A good night's sleep, as you probably know, can make a world of difference in your child's ability to handle himself/herself. It can refuel his/her body's energy, give his/her active brain the rest it needs, and all-around put him/her mentally in a better mood.

On the flip side, a lack of sleep is known to disrupt the body's ability to replenish hormones that affect both physical and mental health. For children experiencing anxiety, poor sleep is linked to learning problems, slower emotional and physical growth, bedwetting, and high blood pressure.

CHAPTER 10:

Why Are Anxious Children Afraid?

C hildren are afraid primarily because they confuse the imaginary with what is real. Children are also likely to develop fears from a stimulus that gave them a nasty surprise or even led to trauma.

For example, a child who was approached by a dog who barked at him/her may develop a fear of dogs. Jung stated that some inborn fears are arising from the collective unconscious (such as fear of the dark, or fear of monsters). Sometimes children learn to be afraid from observing and imitating their parents, who fear something. It is important to note that fear also has a positive side, as a protective survival mechanism making people and children alert, sharpening senses in the face of a threat or danger.

What Do Children Fear?

There are many things that children fear, but some are especially widespread, such as fear of the dark, bad dreams, monsters, animals (real or imaginary), fear of crowds/strangers, of doctors/pain, water/bath, loud noises/thunder, fear of a new place/new environment, fear of death, fear of staying alone/fear of abandonment.

How to Assist an Anxious Child?

1. Understand that your child is genuinely afraid. If you have to, bend down to his/her eye level and take a good look at his/her eyes. You can see the fear. When children are afraid, they tend to stutter, speak rapidly and unclearly.

   They often breathe heavily and rapidly, sweat, cry, experience pains in various places on the body, or develop other syndromes. Young children may temporarily "freeze" and be unable to speak.

2. Take your child's fear seriously, and show empathy to your child, in proportion. For example, tell your child, "I understand that the monster is scaring you. It's OK to be frightened."

3. Avoid mocking your child's feelings (for example, do not tell him/her "It's silly to be afraid of the dark," or, "A cockroach is not at all scary...") because it will only teach him/her it's no used to come over to you when he/she feels unpleasant feelings such as fear.

4. If your child clings to you because he's afraid, allow him/her to have the contact. Don't push him/her off or

tell him/her, "There's nothing to be afraid of." Allow him/her to lean on you.

5. Do not always express identification with your child's fear. Do not always say "I'm also afraid/I used to be afraid of the dark (or of snakes, or...)" because your child may develop a mechanism that will allow him/her to feel it's OK to be afraid only if he/she has the same fears as you. This may make it more difficult for him/her to identify with his/her unique fears and may hurt his/her personal development.

6. Do not keep talking too much about the fear. This may cause your child to use fear to get your attention.

7. Practice relaxation breathing with your child. Breathe deeply together. This will slow down your child's pulse, make him/her calmer, and therefore less threatened.

8. Ask your child to describe the "frightening thing" with specific details. The more the subject of his/her fears is discussed and analyzed, the more familiar it becomes and less frightening. Ask your child for details, such as "How does the monster look? What is scary about it? What kind of voice does the monster have? What color is it?" and the like.

9. Gradually transfer the final responsibility of dealing with the fear to the child, while giving him/her a feeling of security that you're there for him/her. If you over-protect your child at each expression of fear, this will

only reinforce your child's lack of confidence and the perception that he/she is unable to handle fear by himself/herself.

For example, fear of monsters which causes a child to sleep with his/her parents leads him/her to think that his/her parents are the only ones who can help him/her cope with monsters. He/she is likely to conclude that he/she lacks the strength to stand up to the monsters alone.

It is important to transmit gradually the "powers" and ability to address monsters to your child, as well, but calm him/her down by assuring him/her that if he/she needs you, you'll always be there to protect him/her.

10. At the moment of encounter with his/her fear, try to calm your child down while he/she is standing on his/her own, and not being carried by you. Bend down and hug your child. The fact that he/she is still standing on his/her own two feet conveys a covert message to him/her that it's not so bad, and he/she has the capability of "standing up to" the fearful object, without being absolutely dependent on the parent.

11. Try some alternative perceptions to see whether your child can view the "frightening thing" in another light. For example, maybe the monster is spitting fire because it's his/her way of saying he/she is afraid of being alone and wants some friends... or perhaps the dog who is

barking is extremely excited to see children, and he/she is not angry at them.

12. Inquire your child for a few thoughts on how to manage the question of his/her fear. Add some ideas of your own if your child can't think up enough ideas. Would a sword be a good weapon? Or is there a magic word that would make the monster disappear? Maybe you could create an imaginary "good monster" whose job it is to protect your child and overcome any bad monster... See which idea appeals to him/her the most, and take it to the next step.

13. Read some children's stories on the subject. Books can show you and your child another viewpoint on fears and how to cope with them.

Accept Fears, Think Positively, and Get Moving

Toddlers, preschoolers, elementary, and primary school children have different kinds of fears and even though many of those fears may seem silly or hilarious to us, for them, they are legit.

According to expert advice, assuaging our fears and nervousness becomes easier when we learn to accept them instead of shunning them. It also becomes easier to deal with anxiety and stress issues when we nurture a positive state of mind that helps us accept our concerns and tensions, and then learn to respond to them positively—instead of reacting to them—so that we can take the best possible course of action in a given situation.

Since this is how experts advise adults to behave towards their anxious thoughts, we need to motivate our kids to do this as well. Your fears are not evil; they are a part of you.

Talk to your kids about how fears, worries, and anxious thoughts are not evil but just elements of their personality that are waiting for their acknowledgment.

Our fears often turn into anxiety, and then anxiety turns into depression because we disregard them. When a thought or fear overstays its welcome inside your mind, it rattles and shakes quite hard. While you may think ignoring certain thoughts curbs it, it often exacerbates the issue.

Discuss this with your children and then teach them to adopt a more nurturing attitude towards their fears. Every time they feel scared or tensed about something, whether it is a concern about who their new grade 4 teacher will be, why their best friend did not talk to them the entire day, why they cannot approach certain kids they like in school, or anything else, they need to acknowledge that fear. Simply writing down the fear and accepting its existence is sufficient to calm it down.

CHAPTER 11:

Practice Positive Self-Talk and Think Positively for Child Experiencing Panic Attacks

O nce your child acknowledges his/her worries, your child then needs to practice positive self-talk in order to quell the worries. Your kids may find this practice strange at first, but if you practice it yourself first and then encourage them to do it, they will follow suit. To do that, ask your child to write down or verbally state the anxious thought. Simply put, your child needs to acknowledge it as discussed in the previous strategy. Following, inquire your child to think almost why the stress keeps coming up, and after that to make a sensible explanation to counter it.

For instance, if your child's worry has to do with a history assignment not being good, a possible counteractive thought can be, "My assignment is good and I'm sure my teacher will like it." Ask your child to chant that suggestion in a strong and assertive voice so that he/she can successfully talk back to and quell his/her worries. Encourage your child to do this every time a worry upsets him/her. With consistent practice, your child will learn the art of replacing worries and negative thoughts with positive and calming thoughts and practicing positive self-talk.

Respond, Do Not React

Because we react to them, anxiety-triggering thoughts often aggravate and cause us to create mountains out of molehills. Kids behave similarly as well. Your child is likely to dwell in worry for hours not because there is a huge, real issue to worry about, but because your child keeps surrendering to his/her reactive thoughts. Make beyond any doubt your conversation to your kids about how responding to certain considerations declines the circumstance. If your child feels he/she should skip school because he/she fears not winning the debate competition, or if he/she is ready to give up cycling in the park because of his/her fear of dogs, you need to help your child learn how to respond instead of reaction to thoughts.

Talk to your child about how every time we succumb to a reactive thought, we empower the anxious thoughts. Take the conversation a bit further by talking to your child about how power needs to lie with us, and how this can only happen when we respond instead of reacting to thoughts.

- Ask your child to do the following every time a strong, anxiety-triggering thought upsets him/her.
- Acknowledge the thought.

- Engage in positive self-talk.
- Allow the emotion to subside on its own without reacting to it. If you are standing when anxiety kicks in, sit down. If you are sitting, get up and move around.
- Take deep breaths and use any deep breathing technique to curb the strong anxiety attack. Do a few other things to distract yourself from the worries and in order to respond to them effectively.

For instance, your child can:

- Listen to music
- Play some soothing or even an upbeat tune that distracts him/her from his/her worries. Listen to the music for a few minutes and if it is possible, dance to the tune. When we become physically active, we feel more enthusiastic and less perturbed.

Bow down in Child's Pose

The child's pose is one of the finest ways to mitigate emotional exhaustion. Get into the child's pose by kneeling on the floor/yoga mat, and then slowly extend your arms in front. Spread the arms far and wide, and place the forehead gently on the floor.

Keep up this posture for 20 to 30 seconds and hone it a couple of times all through the day, especially each time stress hits you difficult. This pose quickly curbs your anxiety as it grounds you to the element of earth and helps flush out all types of negative energies from inside you.

Push against a Wall

For certain kids, deep breathing does not really work and sometimes may even exacerbate tension. If your child is hyperactive and prone to more agitation when engaged in deep breathing exercises, advise your child to engage in physically active exercises as a way of tackling worries. Advice your child to push hard against the wall and then to hold that pose to a count of 5, 10, and 15. As your child does that, ask him/her to imagine his/her worry moving out of his/her system.

Punch It Out

Hand your child a punching bag and ask him/her to punch away all his/her tensions every time he/she feels anxiety rising strongly. This works well for some kids, as it allows these kids to drain away their tensions through physical activity. When your child feels calmer, he/she can work on the subsequent steps. When it subsides, think of how you felt and what made you feel that way.

Next, think of what you should do to tackle the anxiety most effectively and appropriately. For occasion, in case your child endures from social uneasiness, i.e. he/she is frightened of blending with individuals and frequently separates himself/herself from individuals indeed when he/she does not need to, inquire your child to think of what she/he really needs to do.

Ask your child to list down different ideal ways to tackle the anxious thoughts and the anxiety triggers and then take action accordingly.

Your child then needs to employ different strategies to calm himself/herself down and slowly learn to face his/her fears because this is paramount to curbing anxiety for good.

CHAPTER 12:
Cognitive-Behavioral Therapy (CBT)

What Is CBT?

Cognitive-Behavioral Treatment could be a shape of psychotherapy that centers on how we think, feel, and carry on. These three factors shape who we are, the relationships we have, and how we live our lives. Cognitive-Behavioral Treatment may be a way to assist people to learn to require control of their life and live in arrangement with what things most to them. It has been an effective way to help treat a variety of psychiatric, psychological, physical, and additional health conditions.

Those with a diagnosed medical condition benefit significantly from this form of therapy. The practices, techniques, and tools used in sessions; however, can help benefit just about anyone who is suffering from negative thoughts, behaviors, and emotions. Teens can use Cognitive-behavioral tools to overcome debilitating anxiety, severe depression, or big emotions they are struggling to make sense of. Teens especially can learn valuable skills that they can carry with them for the rest of their lives. This can aid in the success they have in school, work, and relationships.

Cognitive-behavioral therapy focuses on learning to stay in the present moment, set goals, and understand how the thought process affects behaviors. Though it is a short-term treatment, it offers long-term positive results. Through this type of therapy, you learn to reprogram your thinking patterns. You also learn the connections that are made between your emotions, thoughts, and behaviors.

Cognitive-behavioral therapy combines several techniques so that the patient can reach their specific goals. Each session includes reviewing progress or concerns. The patient is then given homework that will help them move forward to overcome that negative or dysfunctional thinking. Cognitive-behavioral therapy is used in varying ways, each focusing on the negative thoughts, behaviors, and emotions that can hold you back.

Currently, the most effective treatment for social anxiety disorder is cognitive-behavioral therapy. Its goal is to help the person change his/her thought patterns so he/she can avoid feeling anxious. It also aims to teach patients how they can react appropriately during situations that may trigger their symptoms.

Therapy sessions may involve real-life exposure or systematic desensitization to feared situations. Through this method, the patient can imagine the situation and work through his/her fears in a relaxed and safe environment. He/she can also devise ways on how to react properly the next time he/she is faced with such a scenario.

When you undergo exposure therapy, a professional counselor will guide you and ask you to visualize yourself being in a situation that you feared.

For instance, if you are afraid of eating in front of other people, you will be asked to imagine yourself eating in public and then eventually go out and do it. You will continue to do this until you are no longer afraid of it.

Aside from exposure therapy, you may also undergo social skills training. It will help you develop the skills that you need in different social situations by role-playing and rehearsing.

As you become more prepared and comfortable with these social situations, your anxiety will be reduced.

You may also go through cognitive rebuilding, which involves learning to determine fearful thinking and improving it. After this therapy, you should be able to deal with social situations better.

Finally, you may undergo symptom management skills. You will be taught how to reduce your stress by controlling your breathing as well as other physical responses towards anxiety.

Clinical evidence and research state that cognitive-behavioral therapy can yield positive results due to its comprehensive nature. Experts agree that it can actually produce permanent changes in people's lives. It is not impossible to overcome social anxiety disorder, even though it requires a lot of persistence and consistency to do so.

Supportive Therapy

Aside from having a one-on-one session with a therapist, you can also undergo group therapy. In group sessions, you will work with other people who also have a social anxiety disorder.

You can either join a social support group or a therapy group. Both groups have a specific purpose in helping people deal with social anxiety disorder.

Most social support groups provide general social support. The members practice behavioral exercises or social activities that may cause anxiety.

Therapy groups, on the other hand, focus on treating social anxiety through cognitive-behavioral therapy in a group setting.

In addition, according to Dr. John Krystal of the Yale University School of Medicine, group treatments for psychiatric disorders such as social anxiety disorder can reduce the costs of treatment and increase access to effective therapy in settings wherein the resources for mental health treatment are limited.

Therapy Groups

When you join a therapy group, you will be taught methods on how to deal with situations that can trigger your symptoms. You will be encouraged to face your anxiety and alter the way you feel and think about particular social circumstances while staying in a safe environment.

Through every group session, you will be given a chance to reinforce the behavioral components of cognitive-behavioral therapy and work through their cognitive changes. You will be allowed to work through your newly learned cognitive procedures by constantly facing situations that you fear until you no longer feel anxious about them.

Social Support Groups

Unlike with therapy groups, the members of social support groups do not necessarily have to be diagnosed with social anxiety disorder alone. Anyone with an anxiety disorder can receive support from the members. When you join a social support group, you will be provided with social support but not specific instructions on how to address the goals of treatment and therapy.

Social support groups can vary. Some have regular meetings at a specific location and have a loose structure. Others meet at different locations and times and do fun social activities together. Many members find it comforting and supportive to mingle with other people who also have a social anxiety disorder because they understand what it is like to have the disorder.

It is ideal for you to join a social support group if you need encouragement and emotional support. In any case, in case you have got a more extreme case of social uneasiness clutter, you ought to look for treatment and connect an organized treatment gather. Once you have become better, you can join a social group.

Benefits

The benefits of Cognitive-Behavioral Therapy are to help you understand your thought process and thought patterns. New patterns are developed by evaluating and assessing past experiences, identifying triggers, and setting goals that will allow you to master your thoughts and live a more fulfilling life.

As a teen, this may sound like a complex process. In this time, it has never been more imperative for high scholars to memorize how to recognize and divert their negative considering. There are many things that Cognitive-Behavioral Therapy can help you manage and take control of such as:

- How to identify your negative thoughts?
- How to process big emotions.

- How to manage anger.
- How to process grief or loss?
- How to overcome trauma.
- How to have better sleep.
- How to work through difficult relationships.

The main benefit; however, is recognizing how your thoughts affect your emotions and behavior. It strives to strengthen your ability to identify negative thoughts and re-program your thought process so that you can handle stress, anxiety, fear, and other challenges better.

Basic Principles

- CBT will help provide a new perspective of understanding your problems.
- CBT will help you generate new skills to work out your problem.
- CBT relies on teamwork and collaboration between the client and therapist (or program).
- The goal of CBT is to help the client become their own therapist.
- CBT is succinct and time-limited.
- CBT is direction-based and structured.
- CBT is based on the present, "here and now."
- Worksheet exercises are significant elements of CBT therapy.

Using Cognitive Rebuilding Skills to Overcome Anxiety

To gain control over your fears, you need to work on overcoming beliefs that fuel your anxiety and beliefs about anxiety itself.

Cognitive rebuilding works well for people with anxiety.

Cognitive rebuilding consists of three steps: Distinguishing your negative considerations, weighing the evidence for and against each thought, and then supplanting unhelpful considerations with a more helpful viewpoint. Asking thoughtful questions helps you take a rational approach.

When challenging a thought, ask yourself the following:

- What would I say to someone else in this situation?
- If I didn't feel depressed or anxious, how would I look at the situation?
- How would someone who isn't depressed or anxious look at the situation?
- Is there any objective evidence that my thought is true?

Cognitive Rebuilding—What Are Your Beliefs about Anxiety?

As you know, beliefs feel very convincing at the moment, especially if you've been relying on them for a long time. But if you want to improve your anxiety, you've got to let them go. This exercise is the first step.

Exercise: Sentence Completion—What Are Your Beliefs about Anxiety?

Complete these sentences:

- If I worry all the time, I'll...
- If I didn't worry, I would...
- Worrying makes me feel...
- I first started having anxiety problems when...

When you completed the exercise above, did any of these beliefs come up?

1. **"If I worry all the time, I'll keep myself safe."** It's true that remaining vigilant can, in some cases, help you identify dangerous situations early. But worrying can't protect you from everything that could go wrong. If you think about the real calamities that have happened in your life, you'll probably realize that worrying would not have prevented them from happening. Most of the time, worrying is a waste of your energy.

2. **"If I worry about the worst-case scenario, I won't be so upset or disappointed when it happens."** Worry cannot protect you from loss or disappointment, and it can't keep bad things from happening.

3. **"It's bad for me to worry so much."** Worry can't make you go mad. Neither can you die from it? Sure, anxiety can be scary, but it won't kill you.

4. **"I'm a born worrier. I'll never be able to get over my anxiety."** Some of us do tend to worry more than others. That's just a fact of life. But we can all choose to face our fears and fix our thinking errors. There's a good reason CBT is so popular with therapists working with anxious clients.

CHAPTER 13:

The Frequently Asked Questions about Empath Healing

M ost anxious children can be by nature empath. Here some insights to understand better if your kid is an empath soul.

Question: How Can One Tell a Person Is an Empath?

Answer: An empath is a person with some natural abilities to feel more than a normal person feels. These people are highly sensitive and aware of their surroundings and the surrounding people. They are wise and normally quiet.

These people tend to understand the surrounding people more than the others by observing their energies and actions, and they feel as they are standing in the shoes of the concerned person and that is why they are known as the ones with an innate sense of love and wisdom which leads them towards empathy.

Question: Are There Any Qualities of Empaths?

Answer: Almost thirty features of an empath are stated some of the major ones collectively from those are being overwhelmed in public places and around people with higher energies, feeling other's emotions as their own, they are highly sensitive introverts, have big hearts, sensitive about the relationships and get overwhelmed easily low self-esteem, have weak boundaries about themselves, go through pains and discomfort, etc.

Question: Is There Any Difference Between HSPs and Empaths?

Answer: The highly sensitive people and empaths have a lot in common, but there are a few differences between these two types of people.

Empaths can absorb the energies of everyone around them no matter where they are from or what they do, and they feel as if they are standing in the shoes of the concerned person while on the other hand, highly sensitive people are sensitive about what they see someone going through or what they hear, they cannot feel on the level of an empath and they do not have the abilities to feel for everything and everyone around on the same high-level empaths feel.

Question: How Do I Detect That I Am an Empath?

Answer: The easiest way of knowing if one is an empath or not is reading different accurate things about empathy and relating oneself to it, and if it does not work, different sites provide tests for analyzing if a person is an empath or not.

These tests can be taken, and the answer can be understood.

Question: Are Empaths Good or Bad in Relationships?

Answer: One of the major traits of an empath is being sensitive and caring which gives the relationships a plus point that empaths can be the most loving, caring, affectionate, understanding, and polite in relationships though relationships for empaths are not an easy task, they can be highly effective if they prove to be a burden for them.

Question: Do Empaths Suffer from Depression and Anxiety More Than Normal People?

Answer: yes, it is observed that the empaths are more likely to go through depression and anxiety episodes. Research says that people who suffer from social anxiety are more empathetic than others; it concludes that socially anxious individuals have more socio-analytic abilities than the surrounding people who become overwhelmed with this information and end up having an anxiety episode.

Question: Is Being an Empath Just a Story Made up in My Mind?

Answer: A book about empathy proves that being an empath is not just in the head of people. It is rather a physical nervous reaction, which is observed in ten to twenty percent of the whole population.

Question: Can I Ever Cure Myself of Being an Empath?

Answer: Empathy is not a virus that can be gone by an antibiotic; it is said that a human being can be evolved into more sensitivity than less. So no one can get completely out of being an empath, but they can be healed with the help of given strategies.

CHAPTER 14:

When Is Professional Help Needed for Your Highly Sensitive Child?

A nxiety does present differently in our younger people. It has much more of a bodily focus component, especially for younger children.

They haven't developed the vocabulary yet to be able to describe their feelings.

And so oftentimes, anxiety will present as a stomachache or a headache or distraction in school. And sometimes you can go down the wrong path diagnostically when you listen to those and take them completely at face value.

Yeah, I was really shocked to hear how common the misdiagnosis was in children who are being brought to a therapist, psychologist, or a psychiatrist for anxiety and ended up getting the wrong diagnosis of ADHD, bipolar disorder, OCD, whatever they are.

What were some of those tips? Well, the first thing is to arm yourself with education. So, you got to make sure you understand when a diagnostic term has been thrown around by a therapist or somebody else that thinks that they know your child.

I've also known that teachers sometimes will diagnose the child and say, "I think your child has ADHD," or whatever term has been thrown around. As a parent, go and do the research and do the research with credible sources. So, get a copy of the DSM - you can buy it. It is expensive, but you can buy the DSM, called the Diagnostic and Statistical Manual of Mental Disorders, that providers used to diagnose a mental condition. But also, there are credible websites, for example, the National Institute of Mental Health. They have some of these listings that are actually accurate to the diagnostic manual. So, arm yourself with that knowledge first, and make sure that you ask your provider who is giving you the diagnosis of what that means.

Ask them to have a direct dialogue with you. Don't just take it at face value. "Well, what does this mean, in general?" And, "what does it mean in my child? Yeah, what are you seeing in my child that makes you think that they have this diagnosis?" And then the follow-up to that is, "how do we address it? What's the treatment plan?" Make sure that you get good answers from that. You also will talk about phobias. Yeah, what is a phobia? A phobia is an irrational fear of really anything under the sun.

There are different types of phobias. There are contamination phobias, animal phobias, and there's a situational phobia. So, there are really four kinds of different categories of phobias that people can have. Children tend to have a lot of object-focused phobias. And often interestingly, also cleanliness, contamination fears. And it's interesting because sometimes phobias are sort of just developmental.

They can be afraid of the monsters under their bed for six months, and that'll go away. But when it doesn't go away, then it's time to seek treatment, especially if it starts to impair the child in their functioning and prevents them from doing the things that they have to do as a child.

What I really enjoyed about this series is that you didn't just say, "Oh, well, if you think your kid has anxiety, you need to take them to a therapist," which is when I think most parents would expect the answer to be x, especially talking to a doctor.

If you gave actionable tips on dialogue with your child, whether they're four years old or 14 years old, what specific questions to ask them to see if they had an anxiety issue or a phobia that required the attention of a professional or if it was something that they could just try to mitigate at home. That's a huge timesaver.

That's a money-saver. Yes. Huge educational developments. Yeah, so many benefits to that. And we don't want to over-pathologies anxiety, which we all feel nervous and anxious sometimes. So, this is a quite common human condition. So what I truly need individuals to know is that some of the time there are things that you just can do at home, evidence-based procedures of adapting that you just can educate your children, and in case they can do it on their possess, they do not truly require treatment. Yeah, and sometimes it's developmental, maybe it's situational.

Maybe it's a particular class at school or a particular person. And once that stressor passes, the anxiety does as well. So, I don't want to make people rush to doctor's offices panicking because they think that their child has a severe anxiety disorder when they maybe don't, even if they are in that space when they recognize this anxiety is getting out of control.

They won't be able to go to school there. They can't sleep. Because they're too anxious. Whatever the symptoms may be, you gave some great advice about finding the right doctor. And my favorite part, enter viewing the doctors. Here's what you had to say about that.

Let's take a look. I want to get it specific here for the parents talking to the therapist, especially when they're still figuring out if it's the right fit or not for their child. What is, let's say, three to five of the questions they've got to ask?

Okay, I would ask what their experiences treating children with problems for a particular age range are. "So, what's your experience treating children with an obsessive-compulsive disorder? Between the ages of five to seven?" Because some people are amazing at treating individuals of different ranges of ages, but maybe not so much for the age of your child. There is a difference, as we talked about, which is why anxiety is son complex; anxiety is a different thing in teenagers, adults, and older adults with anxiety. So, you want to know if they've had some experience and are able to describe it to you.

Another important question is to ask them what kind of theoretical modality they work from, is it play therapy? Is it psychodynamic? Is it social learning? Is it cognitive-behavioral, is it straight behavioral? You want to know where they're going to be taking your child in terms of the techniques that they're teaching them.

Psychodynamic therapy is much more insight-oriented; it may not be appropriate for a younger child. Behavioral Therapy is very appropriate for actual children of all ages, but especially younger children when they need that tangible, immediate outcome to know that they're learning something new.

Well, first you need to talk to the provider who gave the diagnosis, ask them, let them know that you have some concerns that might not be the appropriate diagnosis, and share what those concerns are.

And if you suddenly get a satisfactory answer, and you still have some, just, you know, concerns that maybe it doesn't quite describe your child, the way that you see your child, you should get a second opinion. And I encourage people to be transparent with their primary provider, whoever has been helping them up until this point about that. Yeah, they shouldn't feel like it's a slap in the face if they just want to get a second opinion. It can only help the child more just to get another good professional's eyes on it.

Well, if that option is on the table, you need to make sure that you have researched the medication class as much as possible, so you can ask informed questions of your prescribing provider. If you are seeing a good psychiatrist or somebody else who has a specialty in dealing with mental health-related medications for children, they should also be able to give you some helpful information to let you know what side effects to watch for because children's systems are more sensitive than adults and sometimes different. So, the side effects profiles can be quite different. Yeah, so we want to be careful with that. But we also talked about how important sometimes psychotropic medications can be, especially because it helps them receive therapy more easily, right? It helps them to learn coping strategies more easily.

Conclusion

A ll children are very different, and that is why we make a wide variety of products designed to help them fit in. One of the most common issues parents have is having difficulty getting their children to sleep at night.

There are a lot of things that can cause this issue, including poor sleep habits, short attention spans, anxiety, and even illness.

We know it is hard to deal with a child's anxiety. Sure, we understand that an anxious child can be difficult. But at the anxious child, we know it doesn't have to be that way!

Your children are growing up, and it can be hard to keep up with them. With an anxious child, you may have trouble knowing what to do when he/she gets scared.

You might feel like you're always stressed out, or like you can never get the hang of things. Everybody feels this way now and then. It's normal to feel stressed when you're a parent, but it's not okay to allow your child's anxiety to ruin your day.

Children could be a human being with sentiments and feelings similar to you. They need a firm hand to guide them through the world and teach them how to be a productive member of society. Your child needs you to adore and back each step of the way!

Children may not seem worried about the upcoming event, but they are actually anxious about the event. They may not be able to say their concerns, but they can show you by doing things like sitting in their room and crying.

Printed in the USA
CPSIA information can be obtained
at www.ICGtesting.com
LVHW010345081224
798606LV00003B/692